SOLVING MYSTERIES WITH SCIENCE

GHOSTS AND HAUNTED HOUSES

JANE BINGHAM

Raintree

Chicago, Illinois

© 2014 Raintree
an imprint of Capstone Global Library, LLC
Chicago, Illinois

To contact Capstone Global Library, please
call 800-747-4992, or visit our web site,
www.capstonepub.com

All rights reserved. No part of this publication
may be reproduced or transmitted in any form or
by any means, electronic or mechanical, including
photocopying, recording, taping, or any information
storage and retrieval system, without permission in
writing from the publisher.

Edited by Adam Miller, Vaarunika Dharmapala, and
Claire Throp
Designed by Ken Vail Graphic Design
Original illustrations © Capstone Global Library Ltd
2014
Illustrated by Chris King
Picture research by Mica Brancic
Production by Victoria Fitzgerald
Originated by Capstone Global Library Ltd
Printed and bound in China by CTPS

17 16 15 14 13
10 9 8 7 6 5 4 3 2 1

**Library of Congress Cataloging-in-Publication
Data**
Bingham, Jane.
  Ghosts & haunted houses / Jane Bingham.
    pages cm.—(Solving mysteries with science)
  Includes bibliographical references and index.
  ISBN 978-1-4109-5500-5 (hb)—ISBN 978-1-4109-
5506-7 (pb)
1. Ghosts—Juvenile literature. 2. Haunted houses—
Juvenile literature. I. Title. II. Title: Ghosts and
haunted houses.

  BF1461.B47 2013
  133.1—dc23   2012042239

Acknowledgments
We would like to thank the following for permission
to reproduce photographs: Alamy pp. 18 (© ZUMA
Wire Service), 21 (© North Wind Picture Archives),
24 inset (© Mike Hill), 27 (© M Itani), 43 (© Design
Pics Inc./Olivier Mackay); Corbis pp. 30 (© Hulton-
Deutsch Collection), 38 (© adoc-photos); Getty
Images pp. 20 (The Image Bank/John & Lisa Merrill),
23 (Hulton Fine Art Collection/Apic), 39 (Vetta/
Renee Keith), 41 (Time & Life Pictures); Mary Evans
Picture Library p. 35 inset (Harry Price); Photoshot
p. 34; Shutterstock pp. 4 left (© katalinks), 4 right (©
Annette Shaff), 9 bottom (© Darja Vorontsova), 9
top (© Michael Guggemos), 10 (© dundanim), 10 (©
shtukicrew), 11 (© Dmitrijs Bindemanis), 15 bottom
(© Anan Kaewkhammul), 15 bottom left (© Laurin
Rinder), 15 bottom right (© Kamenetskiy Konstantin),
15 top (© Clive Watkins), 19 (© Richard Laschon),
22 (© imagefactory), 22 background (© BortN66), 24
background (© Natthawat Wongrat), 25 (© Michael
Stokes), 26 (Robert Spriggs), 28 (Linda Bucklin), 29
(Steven Chiang), 31 (Mayer George Vladimirovich),
33 (© Samot), 35 main (© Joe Belanger), 40 (©
BerndtVorwald), 42 (© Jeff Thrower); The Kobal
Collection p. 37 (Columbia).

Background design images supplied by Shutterstock
(© argus), (© Merkushev Vasiliy), (© nutech21),
(© Vitaly Korovin).

Cover photograph of an apparition reproduced
with permission of Getty Images (Vetta/M. Eric
Honeycutt).

Every effort has been made to contact copyright
holders of material reproduced in this book. Any
omissions will be rectified in subsequent printings if
notice is given to the publisher.

Disclaimer
All the Internet addresses (URLs) given in this book
were valid at the time of going to press. However, due
to the dynamic nature of the Internet, some addresses
may have changed, or sites may have changed or
ceased to exist since publication. While the author
and publisher regret any inconvenience this may
cause readers, no responsibility for any such changes
can be accepted by either the author or the publisher.

Contents

Ghosts and Haunted Houses: An Unsolved Mystery

Do you believe in ghosts? Or have you ever felt that a place is haunted? Many people claim that they have seen a ghost. Others describe a range of spooky experiences. Some have sensed the presence of an invisible person, heard weird noises, or felt an ice-cold wind. They have all encountered the paranormal— events that lie outside the range of normal experience and do not have an obvious explanation.

What are ghosts?

People who believe in the paranormal say that ghosts are the spirits of the dead that have returned to Earth to visit the living. These supernatural spirits often take the shape of a man, a woman, or a child. People have also reported seeing ghostly animals, carriages, ships, and planes. Some witnesses have seen a whole army of ghosts marching toward them!

Ghosts are usually harmless, but some apparitions can cause a lot of trouble. Poltergeists are mischievous spirits that torment their victims. A poltergeist may make loud noises, such as knocking or banging. It may hurl objects through the air or even pinch or hit its victims!

▶ Ghosts are often scary-looking figures with pale faces and staring eyes.

Haunted places

Some buildings have a very disturbing atmosphere. In these apparently haunted places, people may hear unexplained crashes, screams, or groans. The lights may flicker and go out, and there may be sudden cold spots and gusts of wind. These spooky effects are not just found in buildings. Railroad stations, roads, and even stretches of ocean can be haunted.

▲ Deserted castles like this are often said to be haunted, but is this simply because they look so spooky?

Can the mystery be solved?

In the first part of this book, you can read some spine-tingling stories of spooky experiences. The second part asks the question: Can science solve the mystery of ghosts and haunted houses?

A HEADLESS QUEEN

Do you have nerves of steel? If the answer is no, stay far away from Blickling Hall, in Norfolk, England, on the evening of May 19. On this fateful date, in 1536, Queen Anne Boleyn met a gruesome death. Even today, over four centuries later, it is said that her restless spirit still returns to haunt the place where she was born.

A QUEEN OR A WITCH?

Anne Boleyn was the second wife of King Henry VIII of England, but her reign as queen did not last long. After just three years of marriage, Anne was accused of being a witch. It was claimed that she had used her evil powers to enchant the king. She was found guilty and was condemned to death in the Tower of London. On a chilly spring morning, Anne walked calmly to her death. She knelt quietly at the executioner's block, and her head was sliced cleanly off her body.

A SPINE-CHILLING SIGHT

Some people say the ghost of Anne Boleyn can still be seen in the Tower of London, but she makes her most dramatic appearance at Blickling Hall. At the stroke of midnight every May 19, witnesses have seen a ghostly carriage thundering up the drive toward the Hall. The carriage is a ghastly sight, with its headless driver and horses. But the most chilling sight of all is its ghostly passenger. Seated inside the carriage is the headless queen, while on her lap she cradles her own head!

A GUILTY FATHER

Anne is not the only ghost to haunt Blickling Hall. Many people claim that they have seen the spirit of her father, Thomas Boleyn. Thomas was desperate to gain power at the royal court, so he encouraged his daughters to flatter King Henry VIII. Henry had a love affair with Mary Boleyn before courting her younger sister, Anne. But while Mary managed to survive the experience, Anne met a tragic end.

AN ENDLESS PUNISHMENT

Some people believe that the spirit of Thomas Boleyn is still being punished for his daughter's death. On the night of May 19, a ghostly figure has been seen driving a horse-drawn carriage over the 12 bridges that lie close to Blickling Hall. According to local legend, the ghost is the guilty spirit of Thomas Boleyn. Every year, on the date his daughter died, his spirit is condemned to ride through the night as a punishment for his sins on Earth.

The screaming queen

Six years after Anne Boleyn was beheaded, King Henry VIII's fifth wife was put to death. Catherine Howard was accused of being unfaithful to the king, and she was executed at the Tower of London. Some people have spotted Catherine's ghost at the Tower, but her spirit is felt most strongly at Hampton Court Palace, where she was imprisoned before her trial.

Queen Catherine was held prisoner in a set of rooms inside the palace until, one day, she managed to escape. Desperately, she raced down a long hallway, searching for her husband to plead for his forgiveness. Sadly, Catherine's freedom did not last long, and she was soon captured and dragged back to prison, kicking and screaming. People say the spirit of the desperate queen still haunts the hallway at Hampton Court. Many witnesses have heard her bloodcurdling screams echoing through the haunted hallway.

THE GHOSTS OF BORLEY RECTORY

Borley Rectory in Essex, England, has many stories of being haunted. From the time the house was built in the 1860s to the day it was burned to the ground in a mysterious fire, it was home to a curious company of ghosts, poltergeists, and supernatural spirits.

A GHOSTLY NUN

The first accounts of strange happenings at the rectory date from the 1860s, when servants reported hearing mysterious footsteps. Then, in the 1900s, a new rector (priest) arrived. It wasn't long before the rector's four daughters spotted the figure of a pale young nun wandering through their garden. The girls all sensed that the nun was very unhappy, but when they tried to approach her, she vanished instantly.

TORMENTED BY SPIRITS

In 1928, Reverend Smith and his wife moved into the rectory. Mrs. Smith set about cleaning the house from top to bottom, but she was not prepared for what she found. Sitting at the back of a neglected cabinet, there was an ancient skull of a young woman. Mrs. Smith ran screaming from the house, and, from that moment on, she was tormented by spirits. Everywhere she went in the house, she heard heavy footsteps following her. Servant bells echoed through the hallways and unexplained lights suddenly appeared in the windows.

THE HORROR GROWS

The Smiths were beside themselves with fear. In a desperate attempt to rid themselves of the ghosts, they arranged for Harry Price, a paranormal researcher, to stay with them at Borley. But this step only made matters worse. As soon as Harry set foot inside the rectory, the supernatural activity reached a new level. Stones were hurled at windows and vases and bottles sailed through the air. Not surprisingly, it wasn't long before the Smiths decided to leave, but the ghosts stayed...

A GANG OF POLTERGEISTS

In 1930, Reverend Lionel Foyster, his wife, Marianne, and their daughter, Adelaide, all moved into Borley Rectory. For the next five years, they endured a terrifying series of events. It seemed that a gang of poltergeists was at work in the house, ringing bells, shattering windows, and writing mysterious messages on walls. One night, Marianne was suddenly hurled out of bed, while Adelaide found herself locked inside a room without any key.

SPEAKING TO SPIRITS

After five years of terror, the Foyster family left the rectory, and some serious investigations began. A researcher named Helen Glanville claimed that she had made contact with two spirits. Glanville said she had spoken several times to a sad young nun, who had once lived in a convent on the spot where the rectory stood. The nun had fallen in love with a monk from a nearby monastery and had been punished by being bricked up alive inside the convent walls.

The second spirit contacted by Glanville was an old man. He warned her that he would set fire to the rectory, and this prediction came true in 1939, when the house was consumed by fire. As the flames raced through the abandoned rooms, a neighbor spotted a pale figure at a window. Could it be—she wondered—the ghostly nun of Borley, waving her final farewell to the world?

FINDING REMAINS

In 1943, the paranormal researcher Harry Price returned to Borley. He uncovered two bones and a holy medal buried in the basement of the burned-out rectory. Price was sure he had found the body of the ghostly nun. But not everyone was convinced. Perhaps the mystery of the Borley ghosts will never be solved...

One researcher...claimed that she had made contact with two spirits.

A HOUSE OF HORROR

In the summer of 1977, an ordinary home in Enfield, in North London, England, became a house of horror, as Peggy Hodgson and her four children were forced to endure a living nightmare...

WEIRD HAPPENINGS

The haunting began one quiet summer evening with loud, repeated knockings on the wall. Then, the children's beds began to jolt violently up and down and furniture started creeping across the floor. The family was terrified, but this was just the start of the horrors. Over the next few days, toys flew through the air, icy breezes raced through house, pools of water appeared on the floors, and small fires broke out without any warning. Even more scarily, the children felt themselves being thrown violently out of their beds.

Peggy was desperate to find a cause for these horrifying events. She called the police, but they were just as puzzled as she was. Soon, police investigators had recorded over 20 events that seemed to have no physical explanation.

SPEAKING FOR THE DEAD

Many of the events took place around 11-year-old Janet. One night, she was strangled by her bedroom curtains. Another day, a neighbor spotted her through her bedroom window, levitating above her bed. Janet also seemed to be able to make contact with the spirits of the dead. Speaking in the deep, harsh voice of an old man named Bill, Janet swore angrily at her astonished family.

A SCARY MYSTERY

Some people believed that Janet was playing tricks, but others were puzzled. They argued that an 11-year-old girl could not possibly be the cause of all the weird events that took place in the house. A medium who investigated the case claimed that the house was haunted by the troubled ghost of "Bill," and his angry feelings were making the bad things happen. But whatever explanation was given, one thing was clear. Anyone who entered the Hodgsons' house had an appointment with fear!

RESURRECTION MARY

If you ever happen to be driving along Archer Road, in Justice, Illinois, keep a lookout for a famous hitchhiker. She will have short blonde hair and will be dressed for a dance, in a white party dress and sparkly dancing shoes.

MARY DISAPPEARS

Over the years, several people have offered a ride to the young hitchhiker, who says her name is Mary. And each time their story is the same. Mary sits silently in the car until the driver reaches Resurrection Cemetery. Then she suddenly asks to be let out and walks through the cemetery gates. The last thing the drivers see of Mary is a small figure in a white dress weaving her way between the graves. They are left feeling stunned and scared. Have they just driven with a ghost?

A TRAGIC STORY

There is a tragic story behind the figure of the ghostly hitchhiker. Back in the 1930s, a young girl named Mary was walking home from a dance alone, when she was suddenly hit by a car and killed on the spot. Mary was buried in Resurrection Cemetery, dressed in her favorite party dress and dancing shoes. But Mary was not destined to lie quietly in her grave. Ever since her burial, more than 70 years ago, Mary's ghost has haunted the stretch of road where she died. The local people have named her "Resurrection Mary."

...Mary was not destined to lie quietly in her grave...

Investigating Ghosts

What is the truth behind the spooky stories of ghosts and haunted houses? Many people have tried to find explanations. In this part of the book, you can read about their theories. You can also discover how the theories stand up to the tests of science and common sense.

A scientific approach

Wherever possible, this book will use the scientific method in order to unravel the mystery of ghosts and haunted houses. See the box on the next page to learn more about the scientific method.

▼ Ghost hunters often claim that they are conducting scientific research, but are their methods really scientific?

THE SCIENTIFIC METHOD

Good investigators follow the scientific method when they need to establish and test a theory. The scientific method has five basic steps:

1. Make observations (comments based on studying something closely).

2. Do some background research.

3. Form a testable hypothesis. This is basically a prediction, or "educated guess," to explain the observations.

4. Conduct experiments or find evidence to support the hypothesis.

5. After thinking carefully about the evidence, draw conclusions.

Ask question

→ Do background research

→ Construct hypothesis

Think! Try again.

→ Test with an experiment

→ Analyze results. Draw conclusion.

→ Hypothesis is true

→ Hypothesis is false or partially true

→ Report results

BELIEVERS, SKEPTICS, AND GHOST HUNTERS

People have a range of responses to ghosts and the paranormal. Some people are believers who are convinced that ghosts exist. Some are skeptics who do not believe in ghosts.

Some skeptics conduct scientific investigations to try to find causes for the strange events that take place in haunted places. They use the scientific method to test the evidence they find. There is also another group of investigators, many of whom are not trained scientists. These "ghost hunters" start their investigations with a belief in ghosts. They call themselves paranormal investigators or parapsychologists, but many are not true scientists who have been trained to use the scientific method.

A very long history

People have been telling ghost stories for thousands of years. The ancient civilizations of Egypt, China, and India all had legends of ghosts and haunted places. The Romans believed in good ancestor spirits, called *lares*, and evil ghosts, called *lemures*. In ancient Norse legends, the spirits of the dead visited Earth in chariots pulled by headless horses. Many American Indians believe that the dead can return to haunt the living, and some Navajo people suffer from "ghost sickness."

Contacting the dead

In the mid-19th century, many people in the United States and Europe became fascinated by the idea of contacting the dead. They attended meetings, known as séances, that were led by mediums—men or women who believed that they had special powers. The medium would enter a trance (a half-conscious state) in order to communicate with the spirit world.

Ghosts today

Ghosts still play an important part in our culture today. Many people enjoy books and movies about ghosts and hauntings, and "ghost hunting" TV programs are watched by millions. According to a survey conducted in 2011, 31 percent of Americans believe in ghosts.

▲ On the Day of the Dead, Mexicans of all ages dress up as skeletons to represent the spirits of their ancestors.

GHOSTS AROUND THE WORLD

All over the world, people hold ceremonies to honor the ghosts of the dead. In Mexico, people celebrate the Day of the Dead—a day when the spirits of dead ancestors are believed to return to Earth. In China, people hold a Hungry Ghost Festival. On this day, food is served at a table set with empty seats for ancestor spirits. In the United States, Europe, and Australia, many people celebrate Halloween. This traditional festival is held on the night of All Hallows Eve, when ghosts are said to roam Earth.

▲ This 19th-century picture shows a spirit appearing at a séance. People who believed that the dead could return to Earth were called spiritualists.

Can You Believe Your Eyes?

Most accounts of ghosts feature a pale figure that is seen briefly flitting through the shadows. But can people be sure that they have seen a ghost? This chapter explores some of the tricks the mind can play.

Seeing things

It is surprisingly easy to mistake reflections, shadows, and other vague shapes for a ghostly figure. Scientific tests have revealed that when people are presented with random visual information, their brains try to create the image of a human face or figure, even though there is nobody there.

▲ If you are already feeling scared, it is easy to imagine that a building is haunted.

◀ John Henry Fuseli painted this version of *The Nightmare* in 1781. Hauntings often take place at night, when the victim is half-asleep.

Hallucinations

Some sightings of ghosts may be the result of hallucinations (images of things that are not really there). There are many possible causes for hallucinations. Use of drugs or alcohol, lack of sleep, feverishness, and mental illness can all stimulate the brain to produce very convincing images that have nothing to do with reality.

Reality or dream?

Sightings of ghosts often happen at night, when people are suddenly woken from sleep. Many scientists claim that people appear to see ghosts because their brain is still in a dreaming state. In the brief period when someone has just woken up, his or her brain is not able to tell the difference between reality and dreams.

SLEEP PARALYSIS

Many people have the scary experience of seeing a ghostly figure while they are lying in bed, but they are unable to move, talk, or scream. This experience can be caused by a medical condition known as sleep paralysis. Scientific tests have revealed that most people experience sleep paralysis once or twice in their lives, and it is very common in people with sleep disorders.

Something in the Air?

Is something strange in the atmosphere of haunted places? This chapter will take a careful look at the evidence produced by surveys of haunted houses and other spooky places.

Electromagnetic waves

Electromagnetic waves are waves of energy that travel through the air. When you listen to the radio, watch TV, or heat up food in a microwave oven, you are using electromagnetic waves. But is there a link between electromagnetism and the experience of being haunted?

Researchers have measured electromagnetic waves in a range of apparently haunted places. They have discovered that the waves in these places are stronger than normal and are also unusually changeable. Professor Michael Persinger, a Canadian expert in neuroscience, has suggested that changing levels of electromagnetism could stimulate the human brain to produce some unusual experiences. Persinger has conducted a set of experiments in which volunteers are exposed to sudden changes in levels of electromagnetism. The volunteers describe a powerful feeling of fear and the sense of a ghostly presence in the room.

▶ Scientists have studied brain scans to discover how people respond to unusual electromagnetic effects.

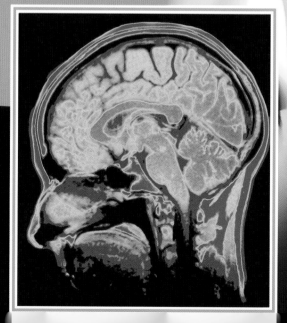

Dry and cold

People staying in haunted houses often describe the experience of feeling suddenly frightened as they enter a "cold spot." But are these cold spots imaginary? Or do they really exist in places that are said to be haunted? Some scientists claim that cold spots may be caused by low levels of humidity (the amount of water in the air). Dr. Richard Wiseman has surveyed several places that are said to be haunted. He has discovered that haunted places have much lower levels of humidity than places where no hauntings have been reported.

ELECTROMAGNETIC TESTS

Scientists have measured electromagnetic levels in different parts of Hampton Court Palace (see page 8). They found the highest levels in the areas where ghosts have been sighted. The areas that were not believed to be haunted had much lower levels of electromagnetism.

Ghosts or infrasound?

Can certain sounds create a sense that a place is haunted? Some sounds are so low-pitched that they cannot be heard by the human ear. This kind of sound, known as infrasound, can be created by distant traffic, thunder, waves, or anything that causes powerful vibrations in the air. Even though the human ear does not register infrasound, the sound waves still create disturbances in the brain. The waves may even cause the human eye to vibrate, making people see things that are not really there.

Scientists have detected infrasound in places that are believed to be haunted. For example, there are very high levels of infrasound in the Edinburgh Vaults in Scotland, caused by the constant rumble of traffic overhead.

▼ The Edinburgh Vaults have a reputation for being haunted. But are these hauntings caused by sound vibrations?

Sound experiment

In 2003, two scientists carried out a fascinating experiment into the effects of infrasound. They organized a concert for 750 people, with music that included passages of infrasound. After the concert, the audience was asked to describe their reactions to the music. Almost a quarter reported unusual experiences when they were listening to the infrasound. Their experiences included getting chills down the spine and feeling nervous, sad, and afraid.

▼ The vibrations caused by infrasound have been proven to produce powerful feelings of fear and distress.

BAD VIBRATIONS

In the early 1980s, Vic Tandy, an engineer, was working in a laboratory. Several people in his lab had reported feelings of fear and unease and a powerful sense that there was some kind of evil spirit in the air. The bad vibrations continued until Tandy noticed a narrow metal blade vibrating slightly. He went in search of the source of the vibration and discovered a damaged extractor fan. As soon as the fan was disconnected, the "bad vibrations" in the lab ceased.

Poison in the air

Is it possible that carbon monoxide gas plays a part in making a house seem haunted? Carbon monoxide is a tasteless and odorless gas that is produced by some household furnaces and boilers. It is highly toxic (poisonous), but its harmful fumes are always directed away from the house through a pipe or chimney.

Symptoms of carbon monoxide poisoning include headaches, nausea (feeling sick), dizziness, and weakness. In some cases, people hear strange sounds and experience hallucinations (see things that are not really there), and they may also have feelings of anxiousness and dread. These symptoms are similar to the feelings reported by people in haunted houses.

▲ Could neglected houses like this have unusually high levels of carbon monoxide gas?

The curious case of Mr. and Mrs. H.

One of the most famous cases of carbon monoxide poisoning happened in Washington, D.C., in 1921. A couple known as Mr. and Mrs. H. moved into a new home, but they soon began to complain of headaches and weakness. They started hearing bells and footsteps at night and even caught glimpses of mysterious figures. Then the couple discovered that previous residents had experienced similar feelings. In fact, their house was believed to be haunted!

The house was thoroughly examined, but no ghosts were discovered. Instead, the furnace was found to be badly damaged, causing carbon monoxide fumes to be forced into the house. Once everything was repaired, the couple recovered completely and did not experience any more ghostly events.

Myth-buster

The ghost in the shower?

In 2005, a 23-year-old woman was found inside her house gasping for breath and in a state of total terror. She claimed she had seen a ghost while she was taking a shower. Later, it was discovered that a new water heater had been installed in her home, and the damaged heater had flooded the house with carbon monoxide when she took a shower.

▶ Was it a ghost or a hallucination in the shower?

Restless Spirits?

Are ghosts restless spirits that are doomed to revisit a place where they once lived? And are some ghosts trying to send a message to the living? This chapter will examine the idea that ghosts return to Earth for a purpose.

Doomed to return?

Many people believe that ghosts return to the place where a dramatic event happened. Often this is the scene of a violent death. For example, it has been claimed that the flickering lights that appear on the side of Brown Mountain in North Carolina are the spirits of American Indians who died in battle. So, is there something special about the atmosphere of haunted places?

Leaving traces?

Some believers in the paranormal claim that very dramatic events leave a "psychic trace" on the places where they happened. They argue that people who see a ghost, or who feel a strong emotion in a certain place, are in fact reading those psychic traces.

In the 1970s, the concept of psychic traces was taken one step further in the Stone Tape theory. According to this theory, ghosts are collections of energy that can be stored in the physical world and then released later, like pressing a button on an old-fashioned tape recorder.

▲ Do the ghosts of people who were wrongly beheaded return as headless ghosts to haunt the living?

▲ Is it possible that some places have a strange atmosphere because of something that happened there in the past?

Myth-buster

Where's the evidence?

Skeptics have questioned the theory of psychic traces. They state that there is no way that this theory can be proven scientifically. The traces cannot be measured by any scientific instruments, and all the evidence for psychic traces is supplied by people who believe in ghosts. This evidence is subjective (based on opinions and beliefs), but scientists only use evidence that is objective (based on facts).

Thought forms

Some parapsychologists have suggested that ghosts are a kind of "thought form" that comes from the mind of somebody who is long dead. They claim that these thought forms are sent out into the atmosphere and then picked up by people in the present day.

Telepathy and science

The theory of thought forms was developed around the end of the 19th century. It is closely linked to ideas of telepathy. People who believe in telepathy claim that thoughts can be sent directly from one mind to another. But many scientists have questioned this claim. They say that the evidence for telepathy does not stand up to the test of the scientific method.

Ghosts or brain waves?

Peter Underwood, a parapsychologist, claims that the theory of thought forms can help to explain why some people see ghostly figures. According to Underwood, people from the past can send out brain waves in the form of electronic pulses. When the brain waves reach a certain level of stress they can produce a ghost, in the form of a telepathic image. Underwood states that mediums are especially skilled at tuning in to telepathic images of ghosts.

▲ The ruined castle at Berry Pomeroy is believed to be home to several ghosts.

HELPING GHOSTS?

In the 1980s, Peter Underwood used a medium to help him make contact with ghosts at Berry Pomeroy Castle in Devon, England. According to Underwood, the ghost of a little girl appeared to the medium. The girl explained that she had been accidentally killed 500 years before and had been wandering around the castle ever since, feeling "bewildered and troubled." Underwood and the medium held a séance to help the spirit of the girl move on. Since then, Underwood claims, the little girl's ghost no longer haunts the castle.

Talking to ghosts?

Is it really possible to talk to ghosts? This is a question that people have been asking for centuries. The belief that people could make contact with spirits was especially strong in the second half of the 19th century, and it continued into the early years of the 20th century. Today, spiritualism had largely died out, but there are still mediums who claim they can talk to ghosts.

Margery and the spirits

In the 1920s, an American spiritualist called Margery became world famous. Margery (whose real name was Mina Crandon) conducted dozens of séances in her home. In these meetings, people sat around a table in total darkness and waited for the spirits to communicate through her. People at the séances reported mysterious crashes and knocks, sudden flashes of light, and strange voices calling out from the shadows. Sometimes the table rose up toward the ceiling, and once a live pigeon appeared in the room.

Margery had many followers, who were all delighted to receive messages from dead relatives and friends. But in 1924, she was exposed as a fraud. Harry Houdini, the famous magician and stunt artist, announced that she had achieved all her effects through a series of tricks.

◄ Harry Houdini discovered that Margery was using a range of tricks. She created wax models of ghostly hands and she secretly pressed a lever under the table to ring a bell in the corner of the room.

HOUDINI

Exposes the tricks used by the

Boston Medium "Margery"

to win the $2500 prize offered by the Scientific American.

Also a complete exposure of

ARGAMASILLA

The famous Spaniard who baffled noted Scientists of Europe and America, with his claim to

X-RAY VISION

PRICE, ONE DOLLAR

◀ Houdini led a campaign to reveal fake mediums like Margery.

THE POWER OF SUGGESTION

One reason why spiritualism proved so popular in the early 20th century was the wish of thousands of people to make contact with the dead. Millions of young soldiers had died in World War I (1914–1918), and the people at séances passionately wanted to receive messages from their loved ones. When people really want to believe something, they are open to the power of suggestion and allow themselves to be convinced that they see or hear something. But scientists learn to question the evidence of their experiences.

Dangerous Energy?

Is it possible that ghosts and poltergeists are the result of powerful energy waves, sent out by troubled people? This chapter will explore this claim.

Psychic energy

Many parapsychologists believe in the power of psychic energy. They claim that people who are very disturbed, angry, or frustrated send out powerful energy waves that have an impact on their surroundings. According to the theory of psychokinesis, a troubled individual can create physical disturbances, causing furniture to move or cups to break.

Teenagers or poltergeists?

The American parapsychologist William G. Roll has investigated many cases of suspected poltergeists. He has concluded that the vast majority of these cases are linked to troubled children and teenagers. Roll believes that these disturbed young people send out waves of negative energy, which has a chaotic effect on their surroundings.

Skeptics say that the children and teenagers in poltergeist cases are in fact doing the damage themselves. Some suggest that the troubled young people may be causing chaos as a kind of cry for help. It is also possible that these disturbed individuals have persuaded themselves that they can really see ghosts.

▲ This photo seems to show a poltergeist at work. But can such evidence be trusted?

JANET AND THE POLTERGEIST

One of the most famous cases of poltergeists centered around 11-year-old Janet Hodgson (see pages 14–15). People who believe in the theory of psychokinesis claim that the weird events in the Enfield house were the result of Janet's psychic energy. But skeptics have put forward a different explanation. They suggest that Janet deliberately created some of the effects. Reporters in the house spotted Janet and her sister bending spoons and deliberately rocking their beds. However, many people believe it was impossible for Janet to have created all the disturbances that took place in her house.

Tricks and Self-Deception

It is surprisingly easy for people to believe that they have had a supernatural experience. This chapter explores some ways that people can be tricked—or can trick themselves—into believing that they have seen a ghost.

Hoaxes and tricks

Some spooky experiences have been proven to be hoaxes. One of the most famous hoaxes was performed by Margery the medium (see pages 34–35). More recently, ghost hunters on TV have been accused of faking their evidence. In a live Halloween program in 2008, one investigator appeared to have his collar pulled down three times by an unseen force. Skeptics claimed that the collar was pulled by a hidden string, but the TV investigators said the action was genuine.

◀ This photograph, taken in 1921, appears to show a medium with the spirit of a dead woman emerging from her head. In fact, the photograph is a hoax.

Truth or legend?

Many sightings of ghosts may simply be a response to a local legend. Once a place has gained a reputation for being haunted, visitors expect to see spooky sights. So it is not surprising that people report seeing ghosts or having creepy feelings. However, believers say that these sightings happen because the place really is haunted!

PHILIP THE IMAGINARY GHOST

Skeptics say that ghosts are produced by the human imagination, but can this claim be proven? In 1972, a group of eight Canadians conducted a fascinating experiment. They invented an imaginary ghost, named Philip Aylesford, who had met a tragic death. Then the group held séances to try to communicate with Philip. In the séances, the ghost of Philip made contact with the group and told them many convincing details about his life as a medieval nobleman. The group reported that the spirit of Philip also appeared to make a table levitate (rise a few inches from the floor).

▲ Can the spirits of the dead really be contacted in a séance?

Physical Causes

Most accounts of haunted houses include descriptions of creepy cold spots, flickering lights, and high-pitched screams and moans. People hear creaking floorboards, crashes, thumps, and knocks. They see vague billowing shapes and are suddenly startled to find a window opening by itself. All these effects can be seen as evidence that a building is haunted, but they can also have physical causes.

Animal noises

Some scary noises heard at night could be caused by animals. Dogs produce long, drawn-out howls, and rabbits caught by foxes squeal loudly in pain. When cats get into a fight, they let out ear-splitting screeches that sound like human screams.

▼ The sound of a dog howling at night can be truly spine-chilling.

Drafts and winds

Drafts from chimneys or windows can cause the temperature in certain parts of a room to drop very sharply. Drafts can also make doors and windows open mysteriously or bang wildly back and forth. Strong winds can produce howling and moaning sounds. The wind can make branches knock repeatedly on windows and make curtains billow in a ghostly way.

Household causes

Central heating and plumbing pipes can produce a range of disturbing knocks, thumps, and gurgles. Changes of temperature inside a building can cause creaking floorboards and can even make objects crash to the ground or slide across the floor. Disturbances in electrical current can cause lights to flicker or go out, while reflections from passing cars can create some spooky lighting effects.

Myth-buster

Freaky photographs

Some people claim that photographs can show evidence of ghosts. They point out unexplained spots of light, sometimes known as orbs. However, skeptics think that orbs have physical causes. They say that orbs may be caused by a camera's flashlight reflecting off specks of dust or moisture in the air. Other possible physical causes are water spots on a camera lens or problems with light sensors.

▶ This photograph of the "Brown Lady" of Raynham Hall, in Norfolk, England, was taken in 1936. Skeptics claim that the ghostly figure was the result of a smudge on the camera lens.

Can the Mystery Be Solved?

People have been scared and puzzled by ghosts for thousands of years. Even today, there are many new reports of ghosts and hauntings. But is there a scientific explanation for ghosts and haunted houses?

ALL SORT OF THEORIES

There are many theories that attempt to explain the mystery of ghosts and haunted places. Some scientists have suggested that ghosts could be optical illusions, hallucinations, or figures seen in a dreaming state. Other experts have conducted scientific investigations of haunted places, measuring electromagnetic energy waves, infrasound, humidity, and carbon monoxide gas.

Parapsychologists have come up with theories of psychic traces, thought forms, and psychic energy waves. On the other hand, skeptics have claimed that ghosts are simply products of the human imagination. Skeptics have also offered some simple explanations for ghostly effects, such as windy weather, animal noises, and noisy plumbing and central heating.

▶ Could ghosts be real? Or do we create them in our imaginations?

LOOKING AT THE EVIDENCE

As you think about all the different theories, try to consider the evidence carefully. Do the theories match up to the test of the scientific method? And do you think their conclusions can be proven scientifically? The subject of ghosts of haunted houses is a complex one, and you will probably decide that several of the theories make sense to you.

▼ Are there good explanations for haunted houses, or will they always be a mystery?

IT'S UP TO YOU

Now that you have considered all the evidence, what do you think about ghosts and haunted houses? In the end, it is up to you to make up your own mind.

Timeline

c. 1000 BCE
People in ancient Egypt, India, and China tell stories of ghosts and haunted houses

458 BCE
The ancient Greek playwright Aeschylus includes a ghost in his *Oresteia* plays

c. 100 CE
The Roman writer Pliny tells a famous story of a haunted house

c. 1600
William Shakespeare writes *Hamlet*, featuring the ghost of Hamlet's father

1813
John Ferriar claims that sightings of ghosts are the result of optical illusions

1820
Washington Irving publishes *The Legend of Sleepy Hollow*, featuring a headless horseman

1839
Edgar Allen Poe publishes *The Fall of the House of Usher*

Alexandre Brierre de Boismont claims that sightings of ghosts are the result of hallucinations

1898
Henry James publishes *The Turn of the Screw*

1900s
The theory of thought forms is developed

1904
M. R. James publishes his first collection of ghost stories

1914
The theory of psychokinesis is introduced

1924
Mina Crandon (Margery the Medium) is exposed as a fake

1920s
Harry Price begins work as a ghost hunter

1940s
Peter Underwood begins work as a ghost hunter

1950s
William G. Roll starts his investigations into poltergeists and psychic energy

1972
The Philip experiment, in Canada, attempts to create an imaginary ghost

1974
Michael Persinger publishes his first findings on electromagnetic waves in haunted places

1977
The case of the Enfield Poltergeist develops

Stephen King publishes *The Shining*

Jay Anson publishes *The Amityville Horror*, a story apparently based on a real-life haunting

1983
Susan Hill publishes *The Woman in Black*

1984
The movie *Ghostbusters* is released. It triggers a craze for ghost hunting.

1990s
Richard Wiseman starts investigating the effects of ultrasound in haunted places

2012
The movie of *The Woman in Black* is released

Summing Up the Science

Some investigators of ghosts and haunted houses measure energy waves (see pages 24–27). But what exactly are these invisible waves that travel through the air?

Energy is produced by a force called electromagnetism. It can take many different forms, including light, heat, and noise. Each energy type travels at a different rate through the atmosphere and sends out waves of a different length. These energy waves are sometimes known as electromagnetic waves, and scientists can measure them very precisely.

Scientists have created a chart showing the range of electromagnetic waves in our atmosphere. This range of energy is known as the electromagnetic spectrum. The diagram below shows a very simplified version of the electromagnetic spectrum. The longest waves are radio waves, which produce sounds. The shortest and most powerful waves are gamma rays, which are used to kill cancer cells.

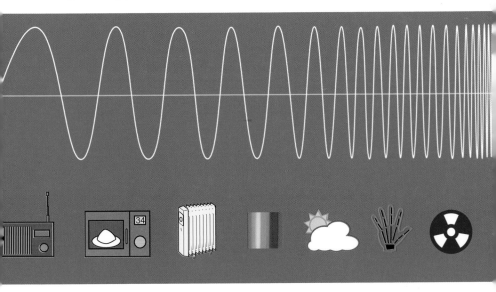

▲ The electromagnetic spectrum ranges from radio waves to gamma waves.

Glossary

apparition something that can be seen, but not explained

atmosphere mood or feeling created by a place; air surrounding Earth

carbon monoxide poisonous gas

condemned forced to do something

convent set of buildings where nuns live

electromagnetic wave wave of energy created by the force of electromagnetism, which has its source in the Sun

hallucination sight that is not really there

hitchhiker person who gets a ride from a driver in a passing car or truck

humidity moisture in the air

hypothesis explanation for an occurrence or problem that needs evidence or testing before it can be accepted as true

infrasound sound that is too low-pitched to be heard by the human ear

levitate rise and hover above the ground

medium someone who claims to communicate with the spirits of the dead

neuroscience scientific study of the brain and the nervous system

optical illusion sight that your eyes trick you into believing is real

paranormal unexplained by normal, everyday causes

parapsychologist someone who believes in ghosts and the supernatural and who conducts investigations into these subjects

poltergeist spirit that has a physical effect on its surroundings

presence sense that something is there, even though it cannot be seen

psychic energy energy created by powerful emotions

psychic trace lasting effects of the energy created by powerful emotions

psychokinesis movements or changes caused by the energy created by powerful emotions

rectory house where a local priest lives

séance meeting in which people try to make contact with the spirits of the dead

sensor equipment that responds to light, sound, touch, and so on

skeptic someone who questions things

spiritualist someone who believes that it is possible to make contact with the spirits of the dead

supernatural beyond the natural, everyday world

telepathy sending information directly from the brain of one person to another, without using speech or writing

thought form idea sent from the brain of one person to another, without using speech or writing

witness someone who describes something he or she has seen

Find Out More

BOOKS

Ganeri, Anita. *Ghosts and Other Specters* (The Dark Side). New York: PowerKids, 2011.

Hawes, Jason, and Grant Wilson. *Ghost Hunt: Chilling Tales of the Unknown*. New York: Little, Brown, 2010.

Hawes, Jason, and Grant Wilson. *Ghost Hunt 2: More Chilling Tales of the Unknown*. New York: Little, Brown, 2011.

Krovatin, Christopher. *The Best Ghost Stories Ever* (Scholastic Classics). New York: Scholastic, 2003.

WEB SITES

www.fst.org/margery.htm
Learn more about Margery, an American medium working in the 1920s, who claimed to be able to communicate with ghosts.

www.hp-lexicon.org/wizards/ghosts.html
Read this guide to ghosts in the Harry Potter books.

paranormal.about.com/od/ghostphotos/ig/Best-Ghost-Photos
Take a look at this gallery of ghost photos and the stories behind them.

www.richardwiseman.com/hauntings2/index.html
Scientist Richard Wiseman reports on experiments into ghosts and haunted houses at this site.

tlc.howstuffworks.com/family/ghost-stories.htm
Discover this collection of scary ghost stories.

TOPICS TO RESEARCH

- The Day of the Dead festival in Mexico
- American Indian beliefs about ghosts
- The history of spiritualism
- Dreams and dreaming states.

Index